A CELEBRATION OF PEACE

HELEN STEINER RICE

BARBOUR
PUBLISHING

A HELEN STEINER RICE * Product

© 2014 by Barbour Publishing, Inc.

Compiled by JoAnne Simmons.

All poems © Helen Steiner Rice Foundation Fund, LLC, a wholly owned subsidiary of Cincinnati Museum Center. All rights reserved.

Published under license from the Helen Steiner Rice Foundation Fund, LLC.

Print ISBN 978-1-62416-646-4

eBook Editions:
Adobe Digital Edition (.epub) 978-1-62836-337-1
Kindle and MobiPocket Edition (.prc) 978-1-62836-338-8

Published by Barbour Publishing, Inc., P.O. Box 719, Uhrichsville, Ohio 44683, www.barbourbooks.com

Our mission is to publish and distribute inspirational products offering exceptional value and biblical encouragement to the masses.

ecpa Member of the
Evangelical Christian
Publishers Association

Printed in the United States of America.

Contents

WHO GOD IS

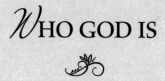

His Likeness
Shines Forth

In everything both great and small
We see the hand of God in all,
And every day, somewhere, someplace,
We see the likeness of His face.
For who can watch a new day's birth
Or touch the warm, life-giving earth
Or feel the softness of a breeze
Or look at skies through lacy trees
And say they've never seen His face
Or looked upon His throne of grace.
And man's search for God will end and begin
When he opens his heart to let Christ in.

Reflections of God's Face

❧

The silent stars in timeless skies,
The wonderment in children's eyes,
The autumn haze, the breath of spring,
The chirping song the crickets sing,
A rosebud in a slender vase
Are all reflections of God's face.

The Earth
Is the Lord's

❧

"The earth is the Lord's and the fullness thereof"—
It speaks of His greatness and it sings of His love.
Through all of creation with symphonic splendor,
God speaks with a voice that is gentle and tender.
And the birds in the trees and the flowers of spring
All join in proclaiming this heavenly King.

Everywhere across the Land You See God's Face and Touch His Hand

❦

Each time you look up in the sky,
Or watch the fluffy clouds drift by,
Or feel the sunshine, warm and bright,
Or watch the dark night turn to light,
Or hear a bluebird brightly sing,
Or see the winter turn to spring,
Or stop to pick a daffodil,
Or gather violets on some hill,
Or touch a leaf or see a tree,
It's all God whispering, "This is Me. . .
And I am faith and I am light
And in Me there shall be no night."

My God Is No Stranger

I've never seen God, but I know how I feel;
It's people like you who make Him so real.
My God is no stranger—He's so friendly each day,
And He doesn't ask me to weep when I pray.
It seems that I pass Him so often each day
In the faces of people I meet on my way.
He's the stars in the heavens, a smile on some face,
A leaf on a tree or a rose in a vase.
He's winter and autumn and summer and spring
In short, God is every real, wonderful thing.
I wish I might meet Him much more than I do;
I wish there were more people like you.

The Masterpiece

Framed by the vast, unlimited sky,
Bordered by mighty waters,
Sheltered by beautiful woodland groves,
Scented with flowers that bloom and die,
Protected by giant mountain peaks—
The land of the great unknown—
Snowcapped and towering, a nameless place
That beckons man on as the gold he seeks,
Bubbling with life and earthly joys,
Reeking with pain and mortal strife,
Dotted with wealth and material gains,
Built on ideals of girls and boys,
Streaked with toil, opportunity's banner unfurled
Stands out the masterpiece of art
Painted by the one great God,
A picture of the world.

The Heavens Declare the Glory of God

❧

You ask me how I know it's true that there is a living God.
A God who rules the universe—the sky, the sea, the sod—
A God who holds all creatures in the hollow of His hand,
A God who put infinity in one tiny grain of sand,
A God who made the seasons—
winter, summer, fall, and spring—
And put His flawless rhythm into each created thing,
A God who hangs the sun out slowly
with the break of day
And gently takes the stars in and puts the night away,
A God whose mighty handiwork defies the skill of man,
For no architect can alter God's perfect master plan.
What better answers are there to prove His holy being
Than the wonders all around us
that are ours just for the seeing.

Only God

At times like these
man is helpless. . .
it is only God
who can speak the words
that calm the sea,
still the wind,
and ease the pain. . .
so lean on Him
and you will never walk alone.

God Already Knows

Beyond that which words can interpret
or theology can explain
The world feels a shower of refreshment
that falls like the gentle rain
On hearts that are parched with problems
and are searching to find the way
To somehow attract God's attention
through well-chosen words as they pray,
Not knowing that God in His wisdom
can sense all man's worry and woe,
For there is nothing man can conceal
that God does not already know. . .
So kneel in prayer in His presence
and you'll find no need to speak,
For softly in silent communion
God grants you the peace that you seek.

We Can't, but God Can

Why things happen as they do
we do not always know,
And we cannot always fathom
why our spirits sink so low.
We flounder in our dark distress;
we are wavering and unstable,
But when we're most inadequate,
the Lord God's always able—
For though we are incapable,
God's powerful and great,
And there's no darkness of the mind
God cannot penetrate. . .
And while He may not instantly
unravel all the strands
Of the tangled thoughts that trouble us,
He completely understands—
And in His time, if we have faith,
He will gradually restore
The brightness to our spirits
that we've been longing for. . .
So remember there's no cloud too dark
for God's light to penetrate
If we keep on believing
and have faith enough to wait.

God's Keeping

To be in God's keeping is surely a blessing,
For though life is often dark and distressing,
No day is too dark and no burden too great
That God in His love cannot penetrate.

The Mystery and Miracle of His Creative Hand

❦

In the beauty of a snowflake
falling softly on the land
Is the mystery and the miracle
of God's great, creative hand.
What better answers are there
to prove His holy being
Than the wonders all around us
that are ours just for the seeing?

Trust God

Take heart and meet each minute
with faith in God's great love,
Aware that every day of life
is controlled by God above. . .
And never dread tomorrow
or what the future brings—
Just pray for strength and courage
and trust God in all things.

He Understands

❧

Although it sometimes seems to us
our prayers have not been heard,
God always knows our every need
without a single word,
And He will not forsake us
even though the way is steep,
For always He is near to us,
a tender watch to keep. . .
And in good time He will answer us,
and in His love He'll send
Greater things than we have asked
and blessings without end. . .
So though we do not understand
why trouble comes to man,
Can we not be contented
just to know it is God's plan?

The Better You Know Him, the More You Love Him!

❧

The better you know God, the better you feel,
For to learn more about Him and discover He's real
Can wholly, completely, and miraculously change,
Reshape and remake and then rearrange
Your mixed-up, miserable, and unhappy life
"Adrift on the sea of sin-sickened strife"—
But when you once know this "Man of goodwill,"
He will calm your life and say, "Peace, be still". . .
So open your "heart's door" and let Christ come in
And He'll give you new life and free you from sin—
And there is no joy that can ever compare
With the joy of knowing you're in God's care.

OUR FATHER IS ALWAYS NEAR

The Hand of God
Is Everywhere

❧

It's true we have never looked on His face,
But His likeness shines forth from every place,
For the hand of God is everywhere
Along life's busy thoroughfare,
And His presence can be felt and seen
Right in the midst of our daily routine.
Things we touch and see and feel
Are what make God so very real.

I Come to Meet You

I come to meet You, God, and as I linger here
I seem to feel You very near.
A rustling leaf, a rolling slope
Speak to my heart of endless hope.
The sun just rising in the sky,
The waking birdlings as they fly,
The grass all wet with morning dew
Are telling me I just met You. . .
And gently thus the day is born
As night gives way to breaking morn,
And once again I've met You, God,
And worshipped on Your holy sod. . .
For who could see the dawn break through
Without a glimpse of heaven and You?
For who but God could make the day
And softly put the night away?

Daily Prayers Dissolve Your Cares

I meet God in the morning
and go with Him through the day,
Then in the stillness of the night
before sleep comes I pray
That God will just take over
all the problems I couldn't solve,
And in the peacefulness of sleep
my cares will all dissolve.
So when I open up my eyes
to greet another day,
I'll find myself renewed in strength
and there will open up a way
To meet what seemed impossible
for me to solve alone,
And once again I'll be assured
I am never on my own.

Today, Tomorrow, and Always He Is There

In sickness or health,
In suffering and pain,
In storm-laden skies,
In sunshine and rain,
God always is there
To lighten your way
And lead you through darkness
To a much brighter day.

Never Alone

Since fear and dread and worry
Cannot help in any way,
It's much healthier and happier
To be cheerful every day—
And if we'll only try it
We will find, without a doubt,
A cheerful attitude's something
No one should be without—
For when the heart is cheerful
It cannot be filled with fear,
And without fear the way ahead
Seems more distinct and clear—
And we realize there's nothing
We need ever face alone,
For our heavenly Father loves us
And our problems are His own.

It's Me Again, God

◈

Remember me, God? I come every day
Just to talk with You, Lord, and to learn how to pray.
You make me feel welcome; You reach out Your hand.
I need never explain, for You understand.
I come to You frightened and burdened with care,
So lonely and lost and so filled with despair,
And suddenly, Lord, I'm no longer afraid—
My burden is lighter and the dark shadows fade.
Oh God, what a comfort to know that You care
And to know when I seek You, You will always be there.

Put Your Problems in God's Hands for He Completely Understands

Although it sometimes seems to us
our prayers have not been heard,
God always knows our every need
without a single word,
And He will not forsake us
even though the way is steep,
For always He is near to us,
a tender watch to keep. . .
And in good time He will answer us,
and in His love He'll send
Greater things than we have asked
and blessings without end. . .
So though we do not understand
why trouble comes to man,
Can we not be contented
just to know it is God's plan?

Never Be Discouraged

There is really nothing we need know
or even try to understand
If we refuse to be discouraged
and trust God's guiding hand.
So take heart and meet each minute
with faith in God's great love,
Aware that every day of life
is controlled by God above.
And never dread tomorrow
or what the future brings,
Just pray for strength and courage
and trust God in all things.
And never grow discouraged—
be patient and just wait,
For God never comes too early,
and He never comes too late.

God Is Always There to Hear Our Smallest Prayer

❧

Let us find joy in the news of His birth,
And let us find comfort and strength for each day
In knowing that Christ walked this same earthly way,
So He knows all our needs, and He hears every prayer,
And He keeps all His children always safe in His care. . .
And whenever we're troubled and lost in despair,
We have but to seek Him and ask Him in prayer
To guide and direct us and help us to bear
Our sickness and sorrow, our worry and care. . .
So once more at Christmas let the whole world rejoice
In the knowledge He answers every prayer that we voice.

God Will Not Fail You

When life seems empty and there's no place to go,
When your heart is troubled and your spirits are low,
When friends seem few and nobody cares,
There is always God to hear your prayers. . .
And whatever you're facing will seem much less
When you go to God and confide and confess,
For the burden that seems too heavy to bear
God lifts away on the wings of prayer. . .
And seen through God's eyes
earthly troubles diminish,
And we're given new strength to face and to finish
Life's daily tasks as they come along
If we pray for strength to keep us strong. . .
So go to our Father when troubles assail you,
For His grace is sufficient and He'll never fail you.

Thy Will Be Done

God did not promise sun without rain,
Light without darkness, or joy without pain.
He only promised strength for the day
When the darkness comes and we lose our way. . .
For only through sorrow do we grow more aware
That God is our refuge in times of despair.
For when we are happy and life's bright and fair,
We often forget to kneel down in prayer. . .
But God seems much closer and needed much more
When trouble and sorrow stand outside our door,
For then we seek shelter in His wondrous love,
And we ask Him to send us help from above. . .
And that is the reason we know it is true
That bright, shining hours and dark, sad ones, too,
Are part of the plan God made for each one,
And all we can pray is "Thy will be done."
And know that you are never alone,
For God is your Father and you're one of His own.

He Loves You

It's amazing and incredible,
but it's as true as it can be—
God loves and understands us all,
and that means you and me.
His grace is all-sufficient
for both the young and old,
For the lonely and the timid,
for the brash and for the bold.
His love knows no exceptions,
so never feel excluded;
No matter who or what you are,
your name has been included. . .
And no matter what your past has been,
trust God to understand,
And no matter what your problem is,
just place it in His hand. . .
For in all our unloveliness
this great God loves us still—
He loved us since the world began,
and what's more, He always will!

God Is Never
beyond Our Reach

❧

No one ever sought the Father
and found He was not there,
And no burden is too heavy to be lightened by a prayer.
No problem is too intricate, and no sorrow that we face
Is too deep and devastating to be softened by His grace.
No trials and tribulations are beyond what we can bear
If we share them with our Father
as we talk to Him in prayer. . .
And men of every color, every race, and every creed
Have but to seek the Father
in their deepest hour of need.
God asks for no credentials—
He accepts us with our flaws.
He is kind and understanding
and He welcomes us because
We are His erring children and He loves us, every one,
And He freely and completely
forgives all that we have done,
Asking only if we're ready to follow where He leads,
Content that in His wisdom
He will answer all our needs.

WITH GRATITUDE

A Thankful Heart

Take nothing for granted, for whenever you do,
The joy of enjoying is lessened for you.
For we rob our own lives much more than we know
When we fail to respond or in any way show
Our thanks for the blessings that daily are ours—
The warmth of the sun, the fragrance of flowers,
The beauty of twilight, the freshness of dawn,
The coolness of dew on a green velvet lawn,
The kind little deeds so thoughtfully done,
The favors of friends and the love that someone
Unselfishly gives us in a myriad of ways,
Expecting no payment and no words of praise.
Oh, great is our loss when we no longer find
A thankful response to things of this kind.
For the joy of enjoying and the fullness of living
Are found in the heart that is filled with thanksgiving.

Things to Be Thankful For

❧

The good, green earth beneath our feet,
The air we breathe, the food we eat,
Some work to do, a goal to win,
A hidden longing deep within
That spurs us on to bigger things
And helps us meet what each day brings—
All these things and many more
Are things we should be thankful for. . .
And most of all, our thankful prayers
Should rise to God because He cares.

A Heart Full of Thanksgiving

❦

Everyone needs someone to be thankful for,
And each day of life we are aware of this more,
For the joy of enjoying and the fullness of living
Are found only in hearts that are filled with thanksgiving.

Thank You, God, for Everything

Thank You, God, for everything—
the big things and the small—
For every good gift comes from God,
the giver of them all,
And all too often we accept without
any thanks or praise
The gifts God sends as blessings
each day in many ways.
And so at this time we offer up a prayer
To thank You, God, for giving us
a lot more than our share.
First, thank You for the little things
that often come our way—
The things we take for granted
and don't mention when we pray—

The unexpected courtesy,
the thoughtful, kindly deed,
A hand reached out to help us
in the time of sudden need.
Oh, make us more aware, dear God,
of little daily graces
That come to us with sweet surprise
from never-dreamed-of places.
Then thank You for the miracles
we are much too blind to see,
And give us new awareness of our
many gifts from Thee.
And help us to remember that
the key to life and living
Is to make each prayer a prayer of thanks
and each day a day of thanksgiving.

So Many Reasons
to Love the Lord

❧

Thank You, God, for little things
that come unexpectedly
To brighten up a dreary day
that dawned so dismally.
Thank You, God, for sending
a happy thought my way
To blot out my depression on a disappointing day.
Thank You, God, for brushing
the dark clouds from my mind
And leaving only sunshine and joy of heart behind.
Oh God, the list is endless
of the things to thank You for,
But I take them all for granted
and unconsciously ignore
That everything I think or do,
each movement that I make,
Each measured, rhythmic heartbeat,
each breath of life I take
Is something You have given me
for which there is no way
For me in all my smallness to in any way repay.

Make Your Day Bright by Thinking Right

Don't start you day by supposin'
that trouble is just ahead.
It's better to stop supposin'
and start with a prayer instead.
And make it a prayer of thanksgiving
for the wonderful things God has wrought,
Like the beautiful sunrise and sunset—
God's gifts that are free and not bought.
For what is the use of supposin'
that dire things could happen to you,
Worrying about some misfortune
that seldom if ever comes true.
But instead of just idle supposin',
step forward to meet each new day
Secure in the knowledge God's near you
to lead you each step of the way.
For supposin' the worst things will happen
only helps to make them come true,
And you darken the bright, happy moments
that the dear Lord has given to you.
So if you desire to be happy
and get rid of the misery of dread,
Just give up supposin' the worst things
and look for the best things instead.

Showers of Blessings

Each day there are showers of blessings
sent from the Father above,
For God is a great, lavish giver,
and there is no end to His love.
And His grace is more than sufficient,
His mercy is boundless and deep,
And His infinite blessings are countless,
and all this we're given to keep
If we but seek God and find Him
and ask for a bounteous measure
Of this wholly immeasurable offering
from God's inexhaustible treasure.
For no matter how big man's dreams are,
God's blessings are infinitely more,
For always God's giving is greater
than what man is asking for.

A Sure Way to a Happy Day

✧

Happiness is something we create in our minds;
It's not something you search for and so seldom find.
It's just waking up and beginning the day
By counting our blessings and kneeling to pray.
It's giving up thoughts that breed discontent
And accepting what comes as a gift heaven-sent.
It's giving up wishing for things we have not
And making the best of whatever we've got.
It's knowing that life is determined for us
And pursuing our tasks without fret, fume, or fuss.
For it's by completing what God gives us to do
That we find real contentment and happiness, too.

Words Can Say So Little

❧

Today is an occasion for compliments and praise
And saying many of the things
we don't say other days.
For often through the passing days
we feel deep down inside
Unspoken thoughts of thankfulness
and fond, admiring pride.
But words can say so little
when the heart is overflowing,
And often those we love the most
just have no way of knowing
The many things the heart conceals
and never can impart,
For words seem so inadequate
to express what's in the heart.

Forever Thanks

❦

Give thanks for the blessings that daily are ours—
The warmth of the sun, the fragrance of flowers.
With thanks for all the thoughtful,
caring things you always do
And a loving wish for happiness
today and all year through!

A Prayer of Thanks

Thank You, God, for the beauty
around me everywhere,
The gentle rain and glistening dew,
the sunshine and the air,
The joyous gift of feeling
the soul's soft, whispering voice
That speaks to me from deep within
and makes my heart rejoice.

CONVERSATIONS
WITH GOD

What Is Prayer?

Is it measured words that are memorized,
Forcefully said and dramatized,
Offered with pomp and with arrogant pride
In words unmatched to the feelings inside?
No, prayer is so often just words unspoken,
Whispered in tears by a heart that is broken,
For God is already deeply aware
Of the burdens we find too heavy to bear. . .
And all we need do is seek Him in prayer
And without a word He will help us to bear
Our trials and troubles, our sickness and sorrow
And show us the way to a brighter tomorrow.
There's no need at all for impressive prayer,
For the minute we seek God He's already there.

The First Thing Every Morning and the Last Thing Every Night

❧

Were you too busy this morning
to quietly stop and pray?
Did you hurry and drink your coffee
then frantically rush away,
Consoling yourself by saying—
God will always be there
Waiting to hear my petitions,
ready to answer each prayer?
It's true that the great, generous Savior
forgives our transgressions each day
And patiently waits for lost sheep
who constantly seem to stray,
But moments of prayer once omitted
in the busy rush of the day
Can never again be recaptured,
for they silently slip away.

Strength is gained in the morning
to endure the trials of the day
When we visit with God in person
in a quiet and unhurried way,
For only through prayer that's unhurried
can the needs of the day be met,
And only in prayers said at evening
can we sleep without fears or regret.
For all of our errors and failures
that we made in the course of the day
Are freely forgiven at nighttime
when we kneel down and earnestly pray.
So seek the Lord in the morning
and never forget Him at night,
For prayer is an unfailing blessing
that makes every burden seem light.

I Think of You and I Pray for You Too

Often during a busy day
I pause for a minute to silently pray.
I mention the names of those I love
And treasured friends I am fondest of—
For it doesn't matter where we pray
If we honestly mean the words we say,
For God is always listening to hear
The prayers that are made by a heart that's sincere.

The Power of Prayer

❧

I am only a worker employed by the Lord,
And great is my gladness and rich my reward
If I can just spread the wonderful story
That God is the answer to eternal glory. . .
And only the people who read my poems
Can help me to reach more hearts and homes,
Bringing new hope and comfort and cheer,
Telling sad hearts there is nothing to fear,
And what greater joy could there be than to share
The love of God and the power of prayer.

Renewal

When life has lost its luster
and it's filled with dull routine,
When you long to run away from it,
seeking pastures new and green,
Remember, no one runs away from life
without finding when they do
That you can't escape the thoughts you think
that are pressing down on you—
For though the scenery may be different,
it's the same old heart and mind
And the same old restless longings
that you tried to leave behind. . .

So when your heart is heavy
and your day is dull with care,
Instead of trying to escape,
why not withdraw in prayer?
For in prayer there is renewal
of the spirit, mind, and heart,
For everything is lifted up
in which God has a part—
For when we go to God in prayer,
our thoughts are rearranged,
So even though our problems
have not been solved or changed,
Somehow the good Lord gives us
the power to understand
That He who holds tomorrow
is the One who holds our hands.

Let Not Your
Heart Be Troubled

❦

Whenever I am troubled
and lost in deep despair
I bundle all my troubles up
and go to God in prayer. . .
I tell Him I am heartsick
and lost and lonely, too,
That my heart is deeply burdened
and I don't know what to do. . .
But I know He stilled the tempest
and calmed the angry sea,
And I humbly ask if in His love
He'll do the same for me. . .
And then I just keep quiet
and think only thoughts of peace,
And if I abide in stillness
my restless murmurings cease.

Talk It Over with God

You're worried and troubled about everything,
Wondering and fearing what tomorrow will bring.
You long to tell someone, for you feel so alone,
But your friends are all burdened with cares of their own.
There is only one place and only one friend
Who is never too busy, and you can always depend
On Him to be waiting with arms open wide
To hear all the troubles you came to confide. . .
For the heavenly Father will always be there
When you seek Him and find Him at the altar of prayer.

Daily Prayers Dissolve Your Cares

❧

We all have cares and problems
we cannot solve alone,
But if we go to God in prayer,
we are never on our own,
And if we try to stand alone,
we are weak and we will fall,
For God is always greatest
when we're helpless, lost, and small. . .
And no day is unmeetable
if on rising, our first thought
Is to thank God for the blessings
that His loving care has brought,

For there can be no failures
or hopeless, unsaved sinners
If we enlist the help of God,
who makes all losers winners. . .
So meet Him in the morning
and go with Him through the day
And thank Him for His guidance
each evening when you pray—
And if you follow faithfully this daily way to pray,
You will never in your lifetime
face another hopeless day. . .
For like a soaring eagle, you, too, can rise above
The storms of life around you
on the wings of prayer and love.

The House of Prayer

Just close your eyes and open your heart
And feel your cares and worries depart.
Just yield yourself to the Father above
And let Him hold you secure in His love. . .
For life on earth grows more involved
With endless problems that can't be solved,
But God only asks us to do our best—
Then He will take over and finish the rest. . .
So when you are tired, discouraged, and blue,
There's always one door that is opened to you
And that is the door to the house of prayer,
And you'll find God waiting to meet you there. . .
And the house of prayer is no farther away
Than the quiet spot where you kneel and pray.
For the heart is a temple when God is there
As we place ourselves in His loving care. . .
And He hears every prayer and answers each one
When we pray in His name, "Thy will be done."
And the burdens that seemed too heavy to bear
Are lifted away on the wings of prayer.

No Prayer Goes Unheard

Often we pause and wonder
when we kneel down and pray,
Can God really hear the prayers that we say?
But if we keep praying and talking to Him,
He'll brighten the soul that was clouded and dim,
And as we continue, our burden seems lighter,
Our sorrow is softened, and our outlook is brighter.
For though we feel helpless and alone when we start,
A prayer is the key that opens the heart,
And as the heart opens, the dear Lord comes in.
And the prayer that we felt we could never begin
Is so easy to say, for the Lord understands
And He gives us new strength
by the touch of His hands.

Wings of Prayer

❧

On the wings of prayer our burdens take flight
And our load of care becomes bearably light,
And our heavy hearts are lifted above
To be healed by the balm of God's wondrous love,
And the tears in our eyes are dried by the hands
Of a loving Father who understands
All of our problems, our fears and despair,
When we take them to Him on the wings of prayer.

BE STILL

A Prayer for Patience

❧

God, teach me to be patient,
teach me to go slow.
Teach me how to wait on You
when my way I do not know.
Teach me sweet forbearance,
when things do not go right,
So I remain unruffled when others grow uptight.
Teach me how to quiet my racing, rising heart,
So I might hear the answer You are trying to impart.
Teach me to let go, dear God,
and pray undisturbed until
My heart is filled with inner peace
and I learn to know Your will.

Listen in the Quietness

❧

To try to run away from life
is impossible to do,
For no matter where you chance to go,
your troubles will follow you;
For though the scenery is different,
when you look deep inside you'll find
The same deep, restless longings
that you thought you left behind.
So when life becomes a problem
much too great for us to bear,
Instead of trying to escape,
let us withdraw in prayer.
For withdrawal means renewal
if we withdraw to pray
And listen in the quietness
to hear what God will say.

Now I Lay Me Down to Sleep

❧

I remember so well this prayer I said
Each night as my mother tucked me in bed,
And today this same prayer is still the best way
To sign off with God at the end of the day
And to ask Him your soul to safely keep
As you wearily close your tired eyes in sleep,
Feeling content that the Father above
Will hold you secure in His great arms of love.
And having His promise, that if ere you wake
His angels reach down, your sweet soul to take,
Is perfect assurance that, awake or asleep,
God is always right there to tenderly keep
All of His children ever safe in His care,
For God's here and He's there and He's everywhere.
So into His hands each night as I sleep
I commend my soul for the dear Lord to keep,
Knowing that if my soul should take flight
It will soar to the land where there is no night.

Learn to Rest

We all need short vacations
in life's fast and maddening race
An interlude of quietness
from the constant, jet-age pace,
So when your day is pressure-packed
and your hours are all too few,
Just close your eyes and meditate
and let God talk to you.
For when we keep on pushing,
we're not following in God's way
We are foolish, selfish robots
mechanized to fill each day. . .
So when your nervous network
becomes a tangled mess,
Just close your eyes in silent prayer
and ask the Lord to bless
Each thought that you are thinking,
each decision you must make,
As well as every word you speak
and every step you take
For only by the grace of God can you gain self-control,
And only meditative thoughts
can restore your peace and soul.

Listen in Silence
If You Would Hear

❧

Silently the green leaves grow,
In silence falls the soft, white snow,
Silently the flowers bloom,
In silence sunshine fills a room.
Silently bright stars appear,
In silence velvet night draws near,
And silently God enters in
To free a troubled heart from sin.

Lives Distressed
Cannot Be Blessed

Refuse to be discouraged,
refuse to be distressed,
For when we are despondent,
our lives cannot be blessed.
For doubt and fear and worry
close the door to faith and prayer,
And there's no room for blessings
when we're lost in deep despair.
So remember when you're troubled
with uncertainty and doubt,
It is best to tell our Father
what our fear is all about,
For unless we seek His guidance
when troubled times arise,
We are bound to make decisions
that are twisted and unwise.
But when we view our problems
through the eyes of God above,
Misfortunes turn to blessings
and hatred turns to love.

Do Not Be Anxious

❧

Do not be anxious, said our Lord,
Have peace from day to day—
The lilies neither toil nor spin,
Yet none are clothed as they.
The meadowlark with sweetest song
Fears not for bread or nest
Because he trusts our Father's love
And God knows what is best.

Anxious Prayers

⁂

When we are deeply disturbed by a problem
and our minds are filled with doubt,
And we struggle to find a solution,
but there seems to be no way out,
We futilely keep on trying
to untangle our web of distress,
But our own little, puny efforts
meet with very little success.
And finally, exhausted and weary,
discouraged and downcast and low,
With no foreseeable answer
and with no other place to go,
We kneel down in sheer desperation
and slowly and stumblingly pray,
Then impatiently wait for an answer
in one sudden instant, we say,
"God does not seem to be listening,
so why should we bother to pray?"

But God can't get through to the anxious,
who are much too impatient to wait,
You have to believe in God's promise
that He comes not too soon or too late,
For whether God answers promptly
or delays in answering your prayer,
You must have faith to believe Him
and to know in your heart He'll be there.
So be not impatient or hasty,
just trust in the Lord and believe,
For whatever you ask in faith and love,
in abundance you are sure to receive.

The Peace of Meditation

So we may know God better and feel His quiet power,
Let us daily keep in silence a meditation hour.
For to understand God's greatness
and to use His gifts each day,
The soul must learn to meet Him in a meditative way.
For our Father tells His children
that if they would know His will
They must seek Him in the silence
when all is calm and still.
For nature's great forces are found in quiet things
Like softly falling snowflakes
drifting down on angels' wings
Or petals dropping soundlessly
from a lovely full-blown rose,
So God comes closest to us when our souls are in repose.
So let us plan with prayerful care to always allocate
A certain portion of each day to be still and meditate.
For when everything is quiet and we're lost in meditation,
Our souls are then preparing for a deeper dedication
That will make it wholly possible to quietly endure
The violent world around us, for in God we are secure.

POWERFUL PRAISE

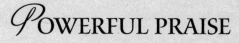

This Is My Father's World

Everywhere across the land
You see God's face and touch His hand
Each time you look up in the sky
Or watch the fluffy clouds drift by,
Or feel the sunshine, warm and bright,
Or watch the dark night turn to light,
Or hear a bluebird brightly sing,
Or see the winter turn to spring,
Or stop to pick a daffodil,
Or gather violets on some hill,
Or touch a leaf or see a tree,
It's all God whispering, "This is Me.
And I am faith and I am light
And in Me there shall be no night."

Expectation! Anticipation! Realization!

❧

God gives us a power we so seldom employ,
For we're so unaware it is filled with such joy.
The gift that God gives us is anticipation,
Which we can fulfill with sincere expectation,
For there's power in belief when we think we will find
Joy for the heart and peace for the mind,
And believing the day will bring a surprise
Is not only pleasant but surprisingly wise.
For we open the door to let joy walk through
When we learn to expect the best, and the most, too,
And believing we'll find a happy surprise
Makes reality out of a fancied surmise.

Show Me the Way

Show me the way not to fortune and fame,
Not how to win laurels or praise for my name,
But show me the way to spread the great story
That Thine is the kingdom and power and glory.

No Favor Do I Seek Today

I come not to ask, to plead or implore You—
I just come to tell You how much I adore You.
For to kneel in Your presence makes me feel blessed,
For I know that You know all my needs best,
And it fills me with joy just to linger with You
As my soul You replenish and my heart You renew.
For prayer is much more than just asking for things—
It's the peace and contentment that quietness brings.
So thank You again for Your mercy and love
And for making me heir to Your kingdom above.

Show Me the Way to Serve and Love You More

God, help me in my feeble way
To somehow do something each day
To show You that I love You best
And that my faith will stand each test,
And let me serve You every day
And feel You near me when I pray.
Oh, hear my prayer, dear God above,
And make me worthy of Your love.

A Part of Me

Dear God, You are a part of me—
You're all I do and all I see;
You're what I say and what I do,
For all my life belongs to You.
You walk with me and talk with me,
For I am Yours eternally,
And when I stumble, slip, and fall
Because I'm weak and lost and small,
You help me up and take my hand
And lead me toward the Promised Land.
I cannot dwell apart from You—
You would not ask or want me to,
For You have room within Your heart
To make each child of Yours a part
Of You and all Your love and care
If we but come to You in prayer.

God's Stairway

Step by step we climb day by day
Closer to God with each prayer we pray,
For the cry of the heart offered in prayer
Becomes just another spiritual stair
In the heavenly staircase leading us to
A beautiful place where we live anew. . .
So never give up, for it's worth the climb
To live forever in endless time
Where the soul of man is safe and free
To live and love through eternity.

Beyond Our Asking

More than hearts can imagine or minds comprehend,
God's bountiful gifts are ours without end.
We ask for a cupful when the vast sea is ours,
We pick a small rosebud from a garden of flowers,
We reach for a sunbeam but the sun still abides,
We draw one short breath but there's air on all sides.
Whatever we ask for falls short of God's giving,
For His greatness exceeds every facet of living,
And always God's ready and eager and willing

To pour out His mercy, completely fulfilling
All of man's needs for peace, joy, and rest,
For God gives His children whatever is best.
Just give Him a chance to open His treasures,
And He'll fill your life with unfathomable pleasures—
Pleasures that never grow worn out and faded
And leave us depleted, disillusioned, and jaded—
For God has a storehouse just filled to the brim
With all that man needs if we'll only ask Him.

God Loves Us

We are all God's children and He loves us, every one.
He freely and completely
forgives all that we have done,
Asking only if we're ready to follow where He leads,
Content that in His wisdom
He will answer all our needs.

God's Love

God's love is like an island
in life's ocean vast and wide—
A peaceful, quiet shelter
from the restless, rising tide.
God's love is like an anchor
when the angry billows roll—
A mooring in the storms of life,
a stronghold for the soul.
God's love is like a fortress,
and we seek protection there
When the waves of tribulation
seem to drown us in despair.
God's love is like a harbor
where our souls can find sweet rest
From the struggle and the tension
of life's fast and futile quest.
God's love is like a beacon
burning bright with faith and prayer,
And through the changing scenes of life,
we can find a haven there.

Look on the Sunny Side

There are always two sides—the good and the bad,
The dark and the light, the sad and the glad. . .
But in looking back over the good and the bad,
We're aware of the number of good things we've had,
And in counting our blessings, we find when we're through
We've no reason at all to complain or be blue. . .
So thank God for the good things He has already done,
And be grateful to Him for the battles you've won,
And know that the same God who helped you before
Is ready and willing to help you once more.
Then with faith in your heart, reach out for God's hand
And accept what He sends, though you can't understand. . .
For our Father in heaven always knows what is best,
And if you trust His wisdom, your life will be blessed. . .
For always remember that whatever betide you,
You are never alone, for God is beside you.

Love Divine,
All Loves Excelling

᪥

In a myriad of miraculous ways
God shapes our lives and changes our days.
Beyond our will or even knowing
God keeps our spirits ever growing.
For lights and shadows, sun and rain,
Sadness and gladness, joy and pain
Combine to make our lives complete
And give us victory through defeat.
Oh "Love divine, all loves excelling,"
In troubled hearts You just keep on dwelling,
Patiently waiting for a prodigal son
To say at last, "Thy will be done."

HELP FOR
THE HURTING

God's Tender Care

When trouble comes, as it does to us all
God is so great and we are so small—
But there is nothing that we need know
If we have faith that wherever we go
God will be waiting to help us bear
Our pain and sorrow, our suffering and care—
For no pain or suffering is ever too much
To yield itself to God's merciful touch!

It Takes the Bitter and Sweet

❦

Life is a mixture of sunshine and rain,
Laughter and teardrops, pleasure and pain,
Low tides and high tides, mountains and plains,
Triumphs, defeats, and losses and gains,
But always in all ways or some dread affliction,
Be assured that it comes with God's kind benediction,
And if we accept it as a gift of His love,
We'll be showered with blessings from our Father above.

God Bless and Keep You in His Care

There are many things in life
we cannot understand,
But we must trust God's judgment
and be guided by His hand. . .
And all who have God's blessing
can rest safely in His care,
For He promises safe passage
on the wings of faith and prayer.

Somebody Loves You

Somebody loves you more than you know,
Somebody goes with you wherever you go,
Somebody really and truly cares
And lovingly listens to all of your prayers. . .
Don't doubt for a minute that this is not true,
For God loves His children and takes care of them, too. . .
And all of His treasures are yours to share
If you love Him completely and show that you care. . .
And if you walk in His footsteps and have faith to believe,
There's nothing you ask for that you will not receive!

There's Peace and Calm in the Twenty-third Psalm

With the Lord as "your Shepherd"
you have all that you need,
For if you "follow in His footsteps"
wherever He may lead,
He will guard and guide and keep you
in His loving, watchful care,
And when traveling in "dark valleys,"
"your Shepherd" will be there. . .
His goodness is unfailing,
His kindness knows no end,
For the Lord is a "Good Shepherd"
on whom you can depend. . .
So when your heart is troubled,
you'll find quiet, peace, and calm
If you'll open up the Bible
and just read this treasured psalm.

God's Sweetest Appointments

Out of life's misery born of man's sins,
A fuller, richer life begins,
For when we are helpless with no place to go
And our hearts are heavy and our spirits are low,
If we place our lives in God's hands
And surrender completely to His will and demands,
The darkness lifts and the sun shines through,
And by His touch we are born anew.
So praise God for trouble that cuts like a knife
And disappointments that shatter your life,
For with patience to wait and faith to endure,
Your life will be blessed and your future secure,
For God is but testing your faith and your love
Before He appoints you to rise far above
All the small things that so sorely distress you,
For God's only intention is to strengthen and bless you.

Somebody Cares

Somebody cares and always will—
The world forgets, but God loves you still.
You cannot go beyond His love
No matter what you're guilty of,
For God forgives until the end—
He is your faithful, loyal friend. . .
And though you try to hide your face,
There is no shelter anyplace
That can escape His watchful eye,
For on the earth and in the sky
He's ever-present and always there
To take you in His tender care
And bind the wounds and mend the breaks
When all the world around forsakes.
Somebody cares and loves you still,
And God is the Someone who always will.

This Is Just a Resting Place

❧

Sometimes the road of life seems long
as we travel through the years,
And with a heart that's broken
and eyes brimful of tears,
We falter in our weariness
and sink beside the way,
But God leans down and whispers,
"Child, there'll be another day."
And the road will grow much smoother
and much easier to face,
So do not be disheartened;
this is just a resting place.

The Home Beyond

We feel so sad when those we love
Are called to live in the home above,
But why should we grieve when they say good-bye
And go to dwell in a cloudless sky?
For they have but gone to prepare the way,
And we'll meet them again some happy day,
For God has told us that nothing can sever
A life He created to live forever.
So let God's promise soften our sorrow
And give us new strength for a brighter tomorrow.

A Time of Renewal

No one likes to be sick, and yet we know
It takes sunshine and rain to make flowers grow,
And if we never were sick and we never felt pain,
We'd be like a desert without any rain.
And who wants a life that is barren and dry
With never a cloud to darken the sky?
For continuous sun goes unrecognized
Like the blessings God sends, which are often disguised,
For sometimes a sickness that seems so distressing
Is a time of renewal and spiritual blessing.

There Is a Reason for Everything

God never hurts us needlessly
and He never wastes our pain;
For every loss He sends to us
is followed by rich gain.
And when we count the blessings
that God has so freely sent,
We will find no cause for murmuring
and no time to lament.
For our Father loves His children
and to Him all things are plain;
He never sends us pleasure
when the soul's deep need is pain.
So whenever we are troubled
and when everything goes wrong,
It is just God working in us
to make our spirits strong.

A Message of Consolation

❦

On the wings of death and sorrow
God sends us new hope for tomorrow,
And in His mercy and His grace
He gives us strength to bravely face
The lonely days that stretch ahead
And to know our loved one is not dead
But only sleeping out of our sight,
And we'll meet in that land where there is no night.

Eagle's Wings

How little we know what God has in store
As daily He blesses our lives more and more.
I've lived many years and learned many things,
But today I have grown "new spiritual wings,"
For pain has a way of broadening our view
And bringing us closer in sympathy, too,
To those who are living in constant pain
And trying somehow to bravely sustain
The faith and endurance to keep on trying
When they'd almost welcome the peace of dying.
And without this experience I would have lived and died
Without fathoming the pain of Christ crucified,
For none of us know what pain's all about
Until our "spiritual wings" start to sprout.
So thank You, God, for the "gift" You sent
To teach me that pain is heaven-sent.

THE VALUE OF FAMILY AND FRIENDS

The Miracle of Marriage

Marriage is the union of two people in love,
And love is sheer magic, for it's woven of
Gossamer dreams, enchantingly real,
That people in love are privileged to feel.
But the exquisite ecstasy that captures the heart
Of two people in love is just a small part
Of the beauty and wonder and miracle of
That growth and fulfillment and evolvement of love.
For only long years of living together
And caring and sharing in all kind of weather
Both pleasure and pain, the glad and the sad,
Teardrops and laughter, the good and the bad
Can add new dimensions and lift love above
The rapturous ecstasies of falling in love.
For ecstasy passes, but it is replaced
By something much greater that cannot be defaced,
For what was in part has now become whole,
For on the wings of the flesh, love entered the soul.

What Is a Baby?

❧

A baby is a gift of life born of the wonder of love—
A little bit of eternity sent from the Father above,
Giving a new dimension
to the love between husband and wife
And putting an added new meaning
to the wonder and mystery of life.

Mothers Are Special People

Mothers are special people
In a million different ways,
And merit loving compliments
And many words of praise,
For a mother's aspiration
Is for her family's success,
To make the family proud of her
And bring them happiness.
And like our heavenly Father,
She's a patient, loving guide,
Someone we can count on
To be always on our side.

It's So Nice to Have a Dad Around the House

❧

Dads are special people—
no home should be without—
For every family will agree
they're so nice to have about.
They are a happy mixture of a small boy and a man,
And they're very necessary in every family plan.
Sometimes they're most demanding
and stern and firm and tough,
But underneath they're soft as silk,
for this is just a bluff.
But in any kind of trouble Dad reaches out his hand,
And you can always count on him
to help and understand.
And while we do not praise Dad
as often as we should,
We love him and admire him,
and while that's understood,
It's only fair to emphasize
his importance and his worth,
For if there were no loving dads,
this would be a loveless earth.

Motherhood

❧

The dearest gifts that heaven holds,
the very finest, too,
Were made into one pattern
that was perfect, sweet, and true.
The angels smiled, well pleased, and said,
"Compared to all the others,
This pattern is so wonderful,
let's use it just for mothers!"
And through the years, a mother
has been all that's sweet and good,
For there's a bit of God and love
in all true motherhood.

It Takes a Mother

It takes a mother's love to make a house a home—
A place to be remembered no matter where we roam.
It takes a mother's patience to bring a child up right
And her courage and her cheerfulness
to make a dark day bright.
It takes a mother's thoughtfulness
to mend the heart's deep hurts
And her skill and her endurance
to mend little socks and shirts.
It takes a mother's kindness
to forgive us when we err,
To sympathize in trouble,
and to bow her head in prayer.
It takes a mother's wisdom to recognize our needs
And to give us reassurance
by her loving words and deeds.

To My Sister

If I knew the place where wishes come true,
That's where I would go for my wish for you,
And I'd wish you all that you're wishing for,
For no sister on earth deserves it more.
But trials and troubles come to us all,
For that's the way we grow heaven-tall.
And my birthday prayer to our Father above
Is to keep you safe in His infinite love,
And we both know that gifts don't mean much
Compared to our love and God's blessed touch.

Life Is a Garden

❧

Life is a garden, good friends are the flowers,
And times spent together life's happiest hours. . .
And friendship, like flowers, blooms ever more fair
When carefully tended by dear friends who care. . .
And life's lovely garden would be sweeter by far
If all who passed through it were as nice as you are.

Hope in Friendship

✤

So many things in the line of duty
Drain us of effort and leave us no beauty,
And the dust of the soul grows thick and unswept;
The spirit is drenched in tears unwept.
But just as we fall beside the road,
Discouraged with life and bowed down with our load,
We lift our eyes, and what seemed a dead end
Is the street of dreams where we meet a friend.

The Garden of Friendship

There is no garden
So complete
But roses could make
The place more sweet.
There is no life
So rich and rare
But one more friend
Could enter there.
Like roses in a garden,
Kindness fills the air
With a certain bit of sweetness
As it touches everywhere.

Friends Are Life's
Gift of Love

❧

If people like me didn't know people like you,
Life would lose its meaning and its richness, too. . .
For the friends that we make are life's gift of love,
And I think friends are sent right from heaven above. . .
And thinking of you somehow makes me feel
That God is love and He's very real.

A Friend Is a
Gift from God

❧

Among the great and glorious gifts
our heavenly Father sends
Is the gift of understanding
that we find in loving friends. . .
For in this world of trouble
that is filled with anxious care,
Everybody needs a friend in
whom they're free to share
The little secret heartaches that
ay heavy on the mind—
Not just a mere acquaintance
but someone who's just our kind. . .
For somehow in the generous heart
of loving, faithful friends,
The good God in His charity and
wisdom always sends

A sense of understanding
and the power of perception
And mixes these fine qualities
with kindness and affection. . .
So when we need some sympathy
or a friendly hand to touch
Or one who listens tenderly
and speaks words that mean so much,
We seek a true and trusted friend
in the knowledge that we'll find
A heart that's sympathetic and
an understanding mind. . .
And often just without a word
there seems to be a union
Of thoughts and kindred feelings,
for God gives true friends communion.

Deep in My Heart

Happy little memories
go flitting through my mind,
And in all my thoughts and memories
I always seem to find
The picture of your face, dear,
the memory of your touch,
And all the other little things
I've come to love so much.
You cannot go beyond my thoughts
or leave my love behind,
Because I keep you in my heart
and forever on my mind. . .
And though I may not tell you,
I think you know it's true
That I find daily happiness
in the very thought of you.

PEACE IN EVERY SEASON

The Blessings of God's Seasons

We know we must pass
through the seasons God sends,
Content in the knowledge that everything ends,
And oh, what a blessing to know there are reasons
And to find that our souls
must, too, have their seasons—
Bounteous seasons and barren ones, too,
Times for rejoicing and times to be blue—
But meeting these seasons of dark desolation
With the strength that is born of anticipation
Comes from knowing that every season of sadness
Will surely be followed by a springtime of gladness.

Each Spring God Renews His Promise

Long, long ago in a land far away,
There came the dawn of the first Easter day,
And each year we see the promise reborn
That God gave the world on that first Easter morn.
For in each waking flower and each singing bird
The promise of Easter is witnessed and heard,
And spring is God's way of speaking to men
And renewing the promise of Easter again. . .
For death is a season that man must pass through,
And just like the flowers, God wakens him, too.
So why should we grieve when our loved ones die,
For we'll meet them again in a cloudless sky.
For Easter is more than a beautiful story—
It's the promise of life and eternal glory.

Growing Older Is
Part of God's Plan

❧

You can't hold back the dawn
or stop the tides from flowing
Or keep a rose from withering
or still a wind that's blowing—
And time cannot be halted
in its swift and endless flight,
For age is sure to follow youth
like day comes after night. . .
For He who sets our span of years
and watches from above
Replaces youth and beauty
with peace and truth and love—
And then our souls are privileged
to see a hidden treasure
That in youth escapes our eyes
in our pursuit of pleasure. . .
So passing years are but blessings
that open up the way
To the everlasting beauty
of God's eternal day.

A Time of Many Miracles

Flowers sleeping 'neath the snow,
Awakening when the spring winds blow,
Leafless trees so bare before
Gowned in lacy green once more,
Hard, unyielding, frozen sod
Now softly carpeted by God,
Still streams melting in the spring,
Rippling over rocks that sing,
Barren, windswept, lonely hills
Turning gold with daffodils—
These miracles are all around
Within our sight and touch and sound,
As true and wonderful today
As when the stone was rolled away,
Proclaiming to all doubting men
That in God all things live again.

The Autumn of Life

What a wonderful time is life's autumn,
when the leaves of the trees are all gold,
When God fills each day as He sends it
with memories, priceless and old,
What a treasure-house filled with rare jewels
are the blessings of year upon year,
When life has been lived as you've lived it
in a home where God's presence is near. . .
May the deep meaning surrounding this day,
like the paintbrush of God up above,
Touch your life with wonderful blessings
and fill your heart brimful with His love.

The Soul, Like Nature, Has Seasons Too

❧

When you feel cast down and despondently sad
And you long to be happy and carefree and glad,
Do you ask yourself, as I so often do,
Why must there be days that are cheerless and blue?
Why is the song silenced in the heart that was gay?
And then I ask God what makes life this way,
And His explanation makes everything clear—
The soul has its seasons the same as the year.
Man, too, must pass through life's autumn of death
And have his heart frozen by winter's cold breath,

But spring always comes with new life and birth,
Followed by summer to warm the soft earth. . .
And oh, what a comfort to know there are reasons
That souls, like nature, must too have their seasons—
Bounteous seasons and barren ones, too,
Times for rejoicing and times to be blue. . .
For with nothing but sameness how dull life would be,
For only life's challenge can set the soul free. . .
And it takes a mixture of both bitter and sweet
To season our lives and make them complete.

After the Winter God Sends the Spring

ॐ

Springtime is a season of hope and joy and cheer—
There's beauty all around us
to see and touch and hear. . .
So no matter how downhearted
and discouraged we may be,
New hope is born when we behold
leaves budding on a tree
Or when we see a timid flower
push through the frozen sod
And open wide in glad surprise
its petaled eyes to God. . .
For this is just God saying,
"Lift up your eyes to Me,
And the bleakness of your spirit,
like the budding springtime tree,
Will lose its wintry darkness
and your heavy heart will sing."
For God never sends the winter
without the joy of spring.

There Is No Death

❧

There is no night without a dawning,
no winter without a spring,
And beyond death's dark horizon
our hearts once more will sing.
For those who leave us for a while
have only gone away
Out of a restless, careworn world
into a brighter day
Where there will be no partings
and time is not counted by years,
Where there are no trials or troubles,
no worries, no cares, and no tears.

CHEERFUL GIVING

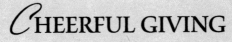

The Blessing of Sharing

Only what we give away
Enriches us from day to day,
For not in getting but in giving
Is found the lasting joy of living,
For no one ever had a part
In sharing treasures of the heart
Who did not feel the impact of
The magic mystery of God's love.
Love alone can make us kind
And give us joy and peace of mind,
So live with joy unselfishly
And you'll be blessed abundantly.

Heart Gifts

It's not the things that can be bought
That are life's richest treasures;
It's just the little "heart gifts"
That money cannot measure—
A cheerful smile, a friendly word,
A sympathetic nod,
All priceless little treasures
From the storehouse of our God—
They are the things that can't be bought
With silver or with gold,
For thoughtfulness and kindness
And love are never sold—
They are the priceless things in life
For which no one can pay,
And the giver finds rich recompense
In giving them away.

Giving Is the Key to Living

❧

Every day is a reason for giving
And giving is the key to living.
So let us give ourselves away,
Not just today but every day,
And remember, a kind and thoughtful deed
Or a hand outstretched in a time of need
Is the rarest of gifts, for it is a part,
Not of the purse but of a loving heart.
And he who gives of himself will find
True joy of heart and peace of mind.

Take Time to Be Kind

❦

Kindness is a virtue given by the Lord;
It pays dividends in happiness and joy is its reward.
For if you practice kindness in all you say and do,
The Lord will wrap His kindness
around your heart and you.

The Joy of Unselfish Giving

Time is not measured by the years that you live
But by the deeds that you do
and the joy that you give. . .
And from birthday to birthday, the good Lord above
Bestows on His children the gift of His love,
Asking us only to share it with others
By treating all people not as strangers but brothers. . .
And each day as it comes brings a chance to each one
To live to the fullest, leaving nothing undone
That would brighten the life or lighten the load
Of some weary traveler lost on life's road. . .
So what does it matter how long we may live
If as long as we live we unselfishly give.

Make Me a Channel
of Blessing Today

❧

Make me a channel of blessing today—
I ask again and again when I pray.
Do I turn a deaf ear to the Master's voice
Or refuse to hear His direction and choice?
I only know at the end of the day
That I did so little to pay my way.

We Meet with Angels Unawares

The unexpected kindness from an unexpected place,
A hand outstretched in friendship,
a smile on someone's face,
A word of understanding spoken in a time of trial
Are unexpected miracles
that make life more worthwhile.
We know not how it happened
that in an hour of need
Somebody out of nowhere
proved to be a friend indeed. . .
For God has many messengers we fail to recognize,
But He sends them when we need them,
and His ways are wondrous and wise. . .
So keep looking for an angel
and keep listening to hear,
For on life's busy, crowded streets,
you will find God's presence near.

Faith to Meet Each Trial

❧

From one day to another, God will gladly give
To everyone who seeks Him and tries each day to live
A little bit more closely to God and to each other,
Seeing everyone who passes
as a neighbor, friend, or brother,
Not only joy and happiness
but the faith to meet each trial
Not with fear and trepidation but with an inner smile.
For we know life's never measured
by how many years we live
But by the kindly things we do
and the happiness we give.

The Richest Gifts

The richest gifts
Are God's to give.
May you possess them
As long as you live,
May you walk with Him
And dwell in His love
As He sends you good gifts
From heaven above.

The Spirit of Giving

⁂

Each year at Christmas, the spirit of giving
Adds joy to the season and gladness to living.
Knowing this happens when Christmas is here,
Why can't we continue throughout the year
To make our lives happy and abundant with living
By following each day the spirit of giving?

The Fragrance Remains

❧

There's an old Chinese proverb
that if practiced each day
Would change the whole world in a wonderful way.
Its truth is so simple, it's easy to do,
And it works every time and successfully, too.
For you can't do a kindness without a reward—
Not in silver nor gold but in joy from the Lord.
You can't light a candle to show others the way
Without feeling the warmth of that bright little ray,
And you can't pluck a rose all fragrant with dew
Without part of its fragrance remaining with you.

Give Lavishly! Live Abundantly!

The more you give, the more you get—
The more you laugh, the less you fret.
The more you do unselfishly,
The more you live abundantly—
The more of everything you share,
The more you'll always have to spare.
The more you love, the more you'll find
That life is good and friends are kind,
For only what we give away
Enriches us from day to day.

INDEX